NO AR

S0-AHG-130

Everything You Need to Know About

AIDS

AIDS can strike anyone.

• THE NEED TO KNOW LIBRARY •

Everything You Need to Know About

AIDS

Barbara Taylor

Series Editor: Evan Stark, Ph.D

THE ROSEN PUBLISHING GROUP, INC.
NEW YORK

Published in 1989, 1992, 1995, 1998 by The Rosen Publishing Group, Inc.
29 East 21st Street, New York, NY 10010

Revised Edition 1998

Library of Congress Cataloging-in-Publication Data

Taylor, Barbara, 1938–
  Everything you need to know about AIDS / Barbara Taylor.
  (The Need to know library)
  Includes bibliographical references and index.
  Summary: Discusses the AIDS disease, its discovery, causes, transmission, treatment, and how to protect oneself from contracting the disease.
  ISBN 0-8239-2833-0
  1. AIDS (Disease)—Juvenile literature. [1. AIDS (Disease).] I. Title. II. Series.
RC607.A26T38 1988
616.97'92—dc19

                                                        88-6579
                                                          CIP
                                                          AC

Manufactured in the United States of America

Contents

Introduction   6

1. HIV and AIDS: A Definition   9

2. How HIV Is Contracted   16

3. How to Prevent HIV Infection   27

4. Testing for HIV   36

5. When You Are HIV-Positive   44

6. Treating HIV and AIDS   48

Glossary   55

Where to Go for Help   58

For Further Reading   60

Index   62

Introduction

*D*onna was sixteen when she started dating Carl.
He was her first boyfriend. They had been going together
for four months when Carl told her he loved her.
Donna was thrilled, and said she loved him too.

They had talked about having sex. But for a long
time Donna didn't feel ready. Donna didn't tell Carl,
but she also was scared about getting AIDS. She knew
that Carl had used steroids last year and shared nee-
dles with other guys on the wrestling team. Carl didn't
use steroids anymore. But what if someone on the
team had passed HIV to him?

Donna was starting to feel ready to have sex with Carl.
But she was still scared and didn't know what to do.

AIDS is a word that frightens almost everyone who
hears it. It's everywhere: in newspapers, on TV, in ads.

You may hear different rumors about AIDS, some of which do not agree with each other. So you might wonder, what exactly is this disease?

AIDS, or acquired immunodeficiency syndrome, is a disease caused by HIV, or human immunodeficiency virus. Like all viruses, HIV is infectious. It travels from person to person. But HIV is contracted only through certain high-risk behaviors, such as having unprotected sex (sex without a condom) or sharing needles with others when using intravenous drugs. It is not spread by having everyday contact, such as hugging, sharing eating utensils with, or drinking from the same water fountain as an HIV-positive person (person who has HIV).

HIV causes AIDS by breaking down the body's immune system, making it unable to fight off disease. A person can be HIV positive for many years and not show symptoms of AIDS. But he or she is said to have AIDS once the immune system starts to fail and life-threatening illnesses set in.

Not everyone who is HIV-positive goes on to develop AIDS. But about half of the people infected with HIV develop AIDS within ten years. And anyone who is HIV-positive can spread HIV, even if he or she feels perfectly healthy.

Unlike with other infections, there are no medicines to cure or prevent AIDS. Recently there have been great developments in managing HIV and preventing AIDS-related illnesses from setting in. But AIDS continues to be a fatal disease. That is why it's so important to learn how to protect yourself.

It is important for information about AIDS to reach everyone because no one is safe from the disease. AIDS strikes both males and females. It strikes people of all races and of all ages. In fact, teens are among the most likely people to contract HIV and develop AIDS. The Centers for Disease Control and Prevention (CDC) estimate that, in the United States, 20 percent of HIV-infected people are teens.

This book will help you understand what AIDS is and what it does to you. You also will learn how to protect yourself from contracting HIV, the virus that causes AIDS. It you have tested HIV-positive, you will learn what steps you can take to prevent the onset of AIDS.

The more you learn about AIDS, the better you can take care of yourself.

Chapter 1

HIV and AIDS:

A Definition

AIDS stands for acquired immunodeficiency syndrome. The name of this syndrome explains a lot about how it works.

Acquired means that you contract the disease. You must take some action to get it—and you can prevent it.

Immunodeficiency is a combination of two words: *immune* and *deficiency.* Immune refers to your immune system, the part of your body that keeps you healthy by fighting off sickness. Deficiency means a lack, or something that does not work properly. So immunodeficiency means an immune system that does not work properly.

A *syndrome* is a set of problems or symptoms associated with a particular illness. Common illnesses associated with AIDS are pneumonia, Kaposi's sarcoma (a type of cancer), and influenza.

HIV and the Immune System

AIDS is caused by HIV, or human immunodeficiency virus. A virus is a tiny semiliving organism that can be seen only under a high-powered microscope. Semi-living means half-alive; that is, a virus is simply tissue when it is outside a body and is alive only when it is inside the body.

A virus grows best inside a living cell. Once the virus enters a body and finds a cell, it enters the cell and lives on that cell's protein. Eventually, as the virus grows and reproduces, the cell is destroyed. The virus then enters new cells. When this happens, the body starts to come down with a disease.

Viruses cause diseases such as colds, mumps, and measles. The immune system often kills viruses even before they make you feel sick.

Scientists have a very hard time studying HIV because it takes many different forms. It changes the way it looks, the way it moves, the way it acts.

In order to understand how HIV works, you first have to understand how the immune system protects us from sickness. Then you can understand why it cannot protect people from contracting AIDS.

A Healthy Immune System

The human immune system usually works so well that we don't even notice it working. It points to viruses, bacteria, even splinters that enter the body. Once an invader (something in the body that should not be there) has been discovered, the system identifies it and

WHAT HAPPENS WHEN A VIRUS ENTERS A PERSON'S BLOODSTREAM

When a virus enters the bloodstream, it is noticed by a T type white blood cell.

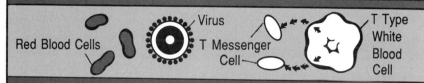

The T type white blood cell sends messages to the T messenger cells.

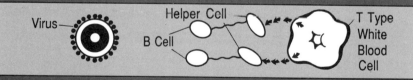

The T messenger cells turn into helper cells and send codes to B cells describing the virus.

B cells make chemicals, called antibodies, which destroy the virus.

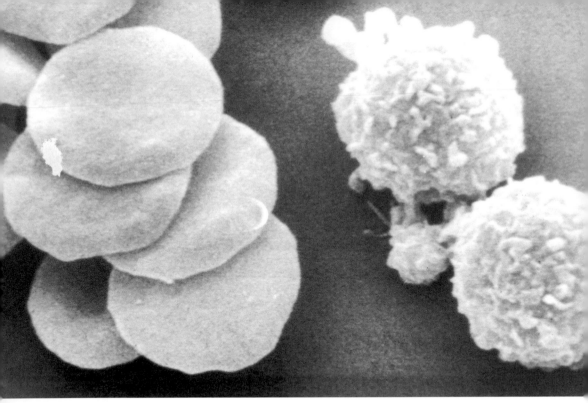

Human blood cells.

then figures out how to defeat it.

The immune system consists mostly of blood cells. There are three kinds of blood cells: red blood cells, which carry oxygen in the blood; platelets, which make clots and scabs when you get a cut; and white blood cells. Only white blood cells help in the immune system process. The white cells come in many different forms. The two most important are T cells and B cells.

The T cells are a kind of alarm system. They sense attacks from bacteria and viruses and send out a warning to the rest of the immune system. The T helper cells pick up the alarm and identify the intruder. They pass this information on to the B cells. The B cells hunt down the infection. When they find it, they make a chemical called an antibody to destroy it. Each infection requires a different antibody to defeat it. The immune system keeps track of which antibody fights which infection. That's why you can get certain infections only once, like chicken pox. The first time you get the infection, the B cells learn which antibody kills the chicken pox infection, so that the next time you are exposed to it the immune system can kill the infection before it makes you sick.

Doctors can help the B cells make antibodies to fight invaders faster. They do this by giving the body an injection of a vaccine. A vaccine contains a small amount of a particular infection—not enough to make you sick, but just enough to make your immune system start producing antibodies. It shows the B cells what antibodies to make. The vaccine helps the B cells "remember" the virus and produce antibodies to defeat it, even years later.

How HIV Attacks the Immune System

HIV wears down your body by attacking the immune system. It attaches itself to T cells and destroys them. As T cells are destroyed, the body is less able to fight off disease.

HIV itself does not kill. However, it leaves the body open to all other infections. Infections that are harmless to a healthy person can cause serious damage to someone who is HIV-positive.

Doctors say that HIV-positive patients are open to opportunistic infections. These are infections that nor-

mally do not attack healthy humans; they take the op-
portunity of attacking humans whose immune systems have already been weakened, such as those with
HIV.

A person who is HIV-positive does not necessarily
have AIDS. He or she will be diagnosed with AIDS
when the T-cell count has dropped below 200 (healthy
immune systems usually have between 800 and 1,200
T cells) or starts showing symptoms of any one of
twenty-six infections that are characteristic of AIDS.

Originally it was thought that HIV multiplies slow-
ly inside the body because it takes many years for a
person to become symptomatic (show signs of disease). However, new research indicates that HIV
"spikes," or sends out billions of cells, when it first
enters the body. Because his or her immune system is
still functioning at first, an HIV-infected person will
not show symptoms right after the spike. But HIV
will wear down the immune system gradually until
symptoms appear.

It's important to study the rate at which HIV multiplies because it affects treatment for HIV. Many treatments now start as early as possible after a diagnosis
of HIV-positive. Many doctors believe there is a chance
that the earlier you start drug treatment for HIV, the
better you can postpone AIDS-related illnesses.

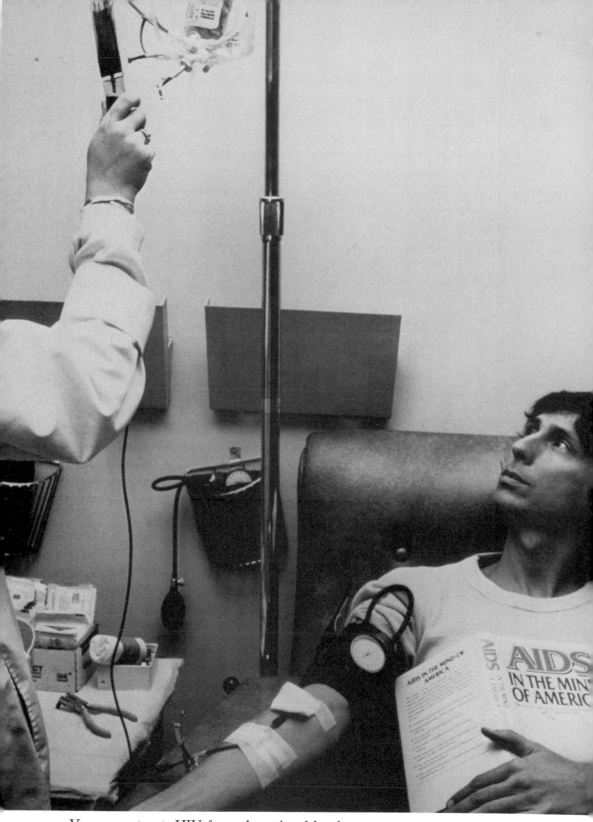

You cannot get HIV from donating blood.

Chapter 2

How HIV Is Contracted

AIDS is a preventable disease. If you take the right precautions, you will not be at risk for contracting HIV, the virus that causes AIDS.

In order to protect yourself, it's important to know the major ways in which HIV is spread.

- Infected blood enters the body through intravenous (IV) drug use;
- During unprotected sex (sex without using a latex condom), infected semen or vaginal fluids enter the body through mucous membranes in the mouth or genitals;
- An infant is infected from his or her mother either before or during birth or from breast milk;
- Infected blood enters the body through a blood transfusion given before 1985. (Hospitals and

blood centers started testing for blood for HIV anti-bodies in 1985).

HIV cannot be transmitted through normal contact with a person: hugging, kissing, holding hands, or sharing eating utensils. It is not transmitted through mosquito bites or through the air. You will not contract it by donating the blood or going to the dentist or doctor.

Next you'll read more about the ways HIV can be transmitted.

Intravenous Drug Use

This year Sherelle started her freshman year at community college. Her best friend Celia went to the same school. They spent at least one night each weekend going to fraternity parties. Although they were under the legal drinking age, Sherelle and Celia had no problem getting beer.

Within a few weeks, Sherelle and Celia got to know some of the brothers at one fraternity pretty well. Paul, Les, and Marcos were like their big brothers. They always brought the girls beer. Sometimes they all sat out on the balcony together and hung out while the party was raging inside.

A few nights, Paul had shared some pot with everybody. He had gotten the drugs from his brother, who had gotten them from someone else. Sherelle liked smoking pot; it made her feel relaxed.

One night when they were all hanging out in Paul's

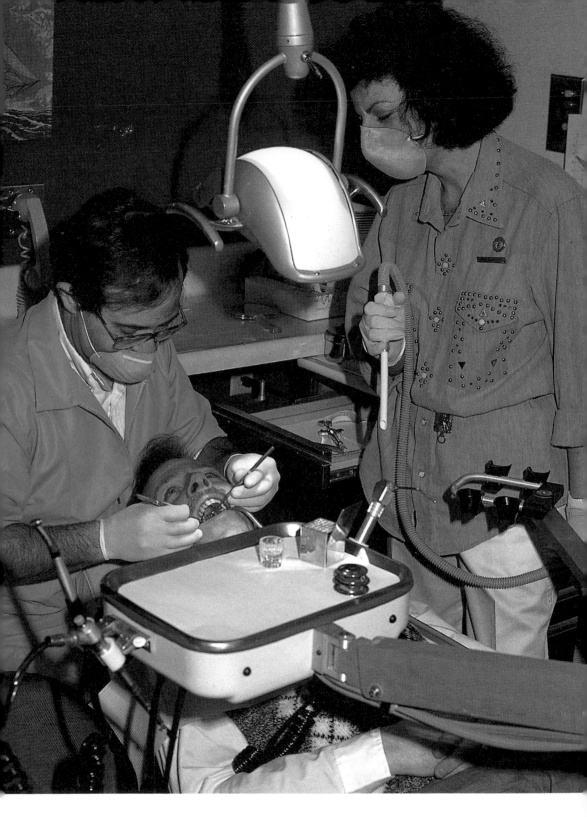

You can't get HIV from going to the dentist or doctor.

room, Paul shut the door. *"Look what I scored,"* he said, and pulled out a syringe from his top dresser drawer.

"What is it?" Sherelle asked.

"It's heroin," Paul said. *"I got it from bro. Precious commodity, but there's just enough to go around for tonight."*

Sherelle and Celia exchanged glances. Sherelle had heard about heroin. It was supposed to give an incredible rush. But she and Celia also had gone to see the movie Trainspotting together. She knew that heroin use could lead to serious trouble.

"I don't know . . ." Sherelle started to say. But before she could finish, she saw Celia injecting drugs into her arm.

Les took the needle from Celia and offered it to Sherelle. *"Next up?"*

Sherelle panicked. She didn't want to try a drug that could really mess you up. And while she knew Celia and the fraternity brothers pretty well, she didn't know if any of them had been tested for HIV. She didn't even know if Celia had been tested.

People who use intravenous drugs such as heroin or steroids are at particular risk of getting AIDS. These drugs are injected into the body with a needle or syringe. Whenever you inject something into your bloodstream with a syringe, a little of your blood remains in the tip of the needle. That blood is inject-ed into the bloodstream of the next person to use the needle. If you are HIV-positive, the person who

Needle-exchange programs have been started so that, if you use intravenous drugs, you don't share needles.

shared your syringe may become infected also.

No one should ever use illegal drugs. However, people who do should make sure never to share used needles. Many cities have needle-exchange programs, by which old needles can be traded for new. If that is impossible, users can clean their needles. Wash out the needle and syringe several times with clean water, then fill them at least three times with full-strength bleach. Rinse them several times again with clean water.

Sexual Intercourse

During sexual activity, both men and women release fluids, and these fluids can contain HIV. Fluids containing HIV can pass through the mucous membranes of sexual partners. If there is a sore or cut in or on the anus, vagina, penis, or mouth, the virus can pass directly from the fluids into the bloodstream through the cut. The cut may not be visible; it may be so small that you don't even know it's there.

HIV can be passed through vaginal, oral, or anal intercourse.

Vaginal Intercourse

Vaginal intercourse is when a man puts his penis into a woman's vagina.

HIV can be transmitted from a man to a woman when pre-seminal fluid (the fluid that comes out of the penis before ejaculation) or semen comes into contact with the mucous membrane of a woman's vagina. It also can be passed from a woman to a man, when the fluids in the vagina come into contact with the mucous membrane of the penis.

Anal Intercourse

Anal intercourse is when a man puts his penis into the rectum (or anus) of a man or a woman. Infected pre-seminal fluid or semen can pass through the mucous membranes of the rectum. Also, the tissues in the rectum are very delicate and can tear easily. Any tears in the lining of the rectum are easy entryways for HIV.

Oral Intercourse

Oral intercourse is when the mouth of a man or woman touches the sexual organs of his or her partner. HIV-infected semen, pre-seminal fluid, and vaginal fluid can pass through the mucous membranes or any cuts or sores in the mouth.

Risks

HIV can be transmitted by sexual activity between a man and a woman, between men, or between women.

All forms of sex carry a risk of HIV transmission. The only certain way to protect yourself from HIV infection is abstinence, or not having sex. Any kind of sex, even protected sex, carries a risk. You have to decide for yourself if you are willing to take that risk.

If you decide to have sex, have safer sex. That means using a latex condom each and every time you have sex.

You will find out more about how to protect yourself from transmitting HIV through sexual intercourse in the next chapter.

Mother to Child

HIV also can be passed from a mother to her fetus (the unborn child in her womb) or to her infant through breast milk.

The baby of a woman infected with HIV will always be born HIV-positive, because it still shares its immune system with its mother. After it develops its own immune system, however, the baby may recover and become HIV-negative.

It takes about eighteen months for an infant to

If you have an HIV test before you get pregnant, you can make sure both you and the baby stay healthy.

develop its own immune system. About one out of four babies remains HIV-positive and dies within a few years. The Centers for Disease Control and prevention (CDC) estimated that by the end of 1997, of all the people living with AIDS in the United States, over seven thousand children were born to mothers with HIV.

If are thinking about having a child, it is important to be tested for HIV. If you test HIV-positive, you will have to think seriously about whether or not you want to have children. Remember that AIDS is a fatal disease. It's possible that you will be ill or will die while your child is still young. According to the CDC, one in every three children orphaned by HIV/AIDS in the United States is under age five. You also may jeopardize the life of your child if he or she remains HIV-positive.

If you already are pregnant, medications such as AZT have been shown to reduce the risk of HIV transmission to a fetus.

Blood Transfusions Before 1985

A transfusion is taking blood from a donor and putting it into another person's bloodstream. A patient may get transfusions during a surgical operation.

Before 1985, there was no test available to detect antibodies to HIV. So if the donor was infected, he or she most likely passed on the virus to whomever received a transfusion.

Hemophiliacs were particularly likely to be infect-

If you have HIV, your blood will be checked regularly for your
T-cell count.

ed in this manner. Hemophiliacs have a blood disor-
der that can be controlled by having regular transfusions. Because hemophiliacs receive transfusions so
often, a high number of them were infected with HIV.

Since 1985, however, all donated blood has been
tested for HIV. It is now very rare to get HIV from a
transfusion.

Chapter 3

How to Prevent HIV Infection

Despite all the news stories about AIDS, most people do not feel affected by it. They think that because of the success of new drugs (called antiretrovials) used to treat HIV, HIV prevention isn't as important anymore. They think that HIV and AIDS will not affect them. They are wrong. New drugs have been helpful in treating HIV, but a cure still has not been found.

Anyone can still get HIV. Age, race, nationality, and sex don't matter. HIV strikes men, women, and children. It strikes rich and poor, famous and unknown, educated and uneducated. There are cases of AIDS in every state in the United States, and around the world.

Control Your Life

You can't tell who has HIV. You can never look at a person and know that he or she is HIV-positive. It

You can't tell just by looking at someone if he or she has HIV.

takes time for the virus to develop in the body. A
person can have HIV for years and never seem sick.
A person can have been exposed to HIV and not
know it.

Until he or she is tested, a person with HIV does
not know that he or she is infected. He or she can
pass HIV to others without knowing it. That is why
HIV prevention is so important at all times.

Sexual Activity

Sexual activity carries with it the danger of HIV
transmission. If you choose to have sex, you must be
as careful as possible.

If you are sexually active, always use a latex condom. It's the only form of birth control that can prevent HIV transmission. A condom is a rubber-like
sleeve that fits over the penis. It is thin and flexible,
but strong. It acts as a barrier between bodies and
bodily fluids.

To use a condom, place it on the tip of the male's
penis. Squeeze the air out of the tip of the condom,
and leave about a half inch of extra space at the tip.
This will catch the male's ejaculation fluid. Without
this little reservoir, as it is called, the condom may
burst.

Pinching the tip, roll the condom back to the base
of the penis. After the male ejaculates, withdraw the
penis and carefully remove the condom.

Use some kind of spermicide containing Nonoxynol-
9 . If you use lubrication, don't use anything petroleum-

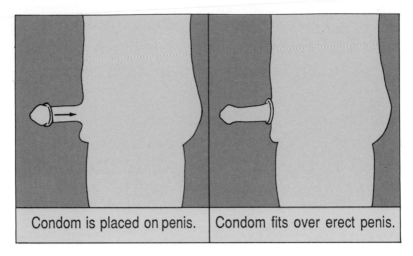

| Condom is placed on penis. | Condom fits over erect penis. |

based; it will destroy the condom. Use KY Jelly or spermicide. Condoms can be used only once.

Condoms can be used for vaginal intercourse, anal intercourse, and oral intercourse (some condoms are even flavored!). You also can use the female condom, which fits inside a woman's vagina.

For oral intercourse on a woman, you can use a dental dam for protection. A dental dam is a piece of latex that can be placed over a woman's genitals to prevent contact between vaginal fluids and the mouth. If you don't have a dental dam, you can make a handy substitute with plastic kitchen wrap (though not the microwaveable kind, because it is too porous to prevent HIV transmission).

The Importance of Communication

Jim has been dating Doreen for a month. They had met at a friend's party and hit it off right away. Since then, they went out for coffee a few times.

Last Saturday Jim invited Doreen over to watch a

Condoms are carefully checked for holes.

movie. It was the first time they were alone. After Jim's parents went to bed, Jim and Doreen started making out.

Doreen pulled away from Jim for a minute. He was sure she was going to ask him to slow down, since they didn't know each other very well. Instead, she told Jim she wanted to have sex.

"You're sure it's okay?" Jim was floored; it was like his wildest dream coming true.

"I'm sure. And don't worry about getting me pregnant," she said. "I'm on the pill."

Jim hadn't planned on going all the way with Doreen yet. But he didn't want to stop.

When Jim and Doreen had sex, both of them were putting themselves in danger. They hadn't even talked about having sex, much less about HIV. While it seems like the least romantic thing to do, talking about HIV with your partner is incredibly important. It can save your life.

Jim was lucky—he didn't contract HIV from Doreen. But a few weeks later, he found out that he had genital herpes, another sexually transmitted disease. Jim didn't know if he had caught it from Doreen or not. He actually may have infected Doreen.

Having sex is a big deal. And it's important to talk about HIV and AIDS with someone before you have sex with him or her. You should know how many people your partner had sex with in the past, and whether or not they had used a condom. The more partners you have unprotected sex with, the greater your risk of being exposed to HIV. You also should know whether or not your prospective sex partner has used intravenous drugs, or has had sex with someone who was a drug user.

Yet it's possible that a person may be HIV-positive and not know it yet. Or he or she may have had unsafe sex or used drugs and won't tell you about it. The only way to be sure is for both you and your partner to be tested for HIV.

Remember, though, that you can be HIV-positive for up to six months before an HIV test actually shows up positive. Many couples get tested together twice—once when they first are thinking and talking about having

If you're in a romantic relationship with another person, it's important to talk about HIV and AIDS.

sex, and again after six months or more have gone by. Then they decide what kind of birth control works best for them.

Having any kind of intercourse always brings the possibility of HIV transmission. But there also are many alternatives to having intercourse. Kissing, hugging, and touching all are safe, so long as you make sure that body fluids don't come into contact with any cuts or sores you have on your skin.

Remember that a condom is the only method of birth control that protects you from HIV. The birth control pill, diaphragm, and the "rhythm method" do not. Withdrawing the penis before ejaculation doesn't, either, because pre-seminal fluid can enter the vagina.

Take your time before deciding to have sex with

33

somebody. It isn't always easy. Many people don't like the idea of waiting to have sex, or of using a condom.

There isn't a surefire way to make someone agree to abstinence or to safer sex. But the important thing is to be sure of yourself—know that you want to be safe. If you are able to talk openly with your partner, you can come to an understanding.

If your boyfriend or girlfriend flatly refuses to have safe sex, you may want to decide whether the relationship is really worth it.

Drug Use

The best way to prevent HIV transmission from intravenous drug use is not to use intravenous drugs. Drugs such as heroin and steroids are injected into a vein in your body. "Skin poppers" are drugs that are injected under the skin. Sometimes people will share their needles. But sharing needles for intravenous drug use is a very easy way to contract HIV.

What's more, using drugs can lead to addiction. A drug can alter your body so that you start to crave larger and larger doses of it. The drug soon becomes the most important thing in your life. When you are addicted to a drug, you lose touch with reality and with people around you. You may not even care anymore if you are exposed to HIV.

Even using non-intravenous drugs can increase your likelihood of contracting HIV. Alcohol or marijuana can affect your judgment. If you are drunk or high, you're more likely to have unsafe sex. And studies have shown that frequent use of drugs such as alcohol weakens your immune system.

It's hard to "just say no" to drugs, especially if you're curious. But the risks and dangers of drug use are very high. It may help to think about how to handle a situation in which you would feel pressured to use drugs. It's possible to say "Sorry, man, not for me" and get off the hook. The key is to be firm and self-assured, and to say no every single time.

If you already are addicted to drugs, try to find a way to stop using. You can find out more about what to do to get and stay off drugs by looking at the resources listed at the end of this book.

Chapter 4

Testing for HIV

*T*ony is scared. In health class last week the teacher talked about how you contract HIV. Since then Tony can't stop thinking about his relationship with his ex-girlfriend Lenore.

Tony and Lenore dated for nearly a year. They had sex without using a condom—Lenore was on birth control pills—although neither of them had been tested for sexually transmitted diseases. Tony said he wanted to marry Lenore, get a job, and start a family. But Lenore said she wasn't ready. A few months after that, Tony and Lenore broke up.

Tony had a hard time getting over Lenore. One afternoon when he was hanging out with his buddy Marco, he felt really down. "I don't know, man," he said. "She was my girl. I would have done anything for her. We could have had a family."

Marco was silent for a minute. "Look, I don't want to burst your bubble," he said cautiously. "But Lenore wasn't all you made her out to be."

"Don't say that." Tony was getting annoyed.

"I'm just saying, that girl may not have been the best thing for you. She was a little messed up in the head, you know."

Tony was getting really mad. "You better tell me why you think that. I'm not just going to sit here and listen to this."

Marco knew it was too late to go back now. "I just know that . . . she was . . . sometimes into drugs and all that. I saw her shoot up at a party right before you met her. And even while you were together, I saw her coked up once or twice."

Tony just sat there, stunned.

"I really didn't want to bring it up. You were so in love, you didn't see it. But now that she's out of your life, just cut your losses and move on."

But Tony couldn't move on. For the next few weeks all he could think about was Lenore. How could he not even notice that she was doing drugs? What was she doing, anyway?

Then came the lesson on HIV and AIDS in health class. Tony was shocked when he realized that he actually was in a "high-risk" category for HIV—Lenore had used intravenous drugs, and he had had unprotected sex with her.

Tony knew he'd better take an HIV test. But he didn't know if he was ready to hear the results.

Testing for HIV is one of the most important steps you can take to protect yourself from AIDS.

If you test HIV-positive, you need to know as early as possible in order to try to prevent AIDS-related illnesses from developing. You also must take care not to spread HIV to others.

If you are HIV-negative, you can plan how to stay HIV-negative by avoiding high-risk behavior.

Who Should Be Tested?

There are some situations at put you in a "high-risk" category for HIV. The two major risks are:

• having had unprotected sex (sex without a condom) with someone; and
• having used intravenous drugs

Yet there are also other situations in which you may want to have an HIV test.

• Consider being tested if you have been sexually abused by someone who is HIV-positive or is at risk for HIV. But whether or not your abuser has HIV, sexual abuse is harmful emotionally as well as physically. Abuse is also against the law. Talk to a teacher, guidance counselor, or another trusted adult who can help you in this situation.

• Consider being tested if one or both of your parents were diagnosed with HIV when you were

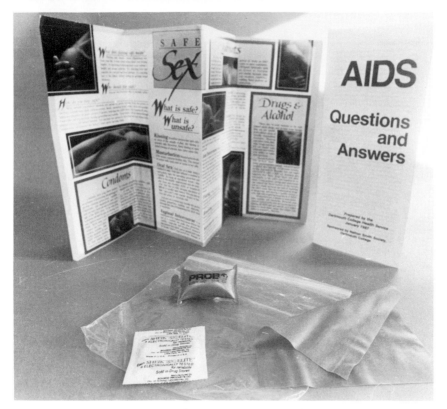

There are many ways to learn about AIDS.

young. In a family, one HIV-positive parent may infect the other parent. And a female can pass it to her unborn child. But you are at risk only if your mother carried the virus while she was pregnant with you. If a parent became infected later, you probably did not contract HIV—you can't contract HIV just by living with someone.

If you fit into one or more of the above categories, you have reason to be tested for HIV. But if you do not fit a high-risk category, it is unlikely that you have HIV.

Yet there are still situations in which you may want to be tested. This is true especially if you are starting a sexual relationship with someone, are planning to have a child, or already are pregnant.

When Should I Be Tested?

HIV testing is important to protect your health. But
before you take the test, take the right steps to pre-
pare yourself.

• Carefully consider where you want to take the test.
  You can be tested by your doctor or at a family
  planning or STD (sexually transmitted disease)
  clinic. Or you can take a home test. In the next sec-
  tion you'll find out more about what each kind of
  testing is like.

• Understand what the test results—both positive
  and negative—mean.
      If you test negative, you can make sure to pro-
  tect yourself from HIV in the future. Also, remember that it's possible to be HIV-positive and still test
  negative. HIV can be in your body for several
  months before it registers as a positive test result.
  You may want to get tested again in six months to
  confirm your HIV-negative status.
      You also need to plan what to do if you test
  HIV-positive. You'll experience a wide range of
  emotions. You'll also have to plan how to take care
  of your health.

• Tell a supportive person—one or both of your parents, a friend, or an adult you trust—that you are

planning to take an HIV test. Ask this person to go with you when you take the test. Taking an HIV test can be stressful and scary, whatever your diagnosis. It's comforting to have someone with you who can help you through it.

Once you have seriously considered these aspects of your HIV test, you should take it as soon as possible.

Testing Procedure

Today there are many options for HIV testing. All of them involve screening a small amount of blood or oral fluid from the mouth. As with any virus, when HIV enters the body, the body produces antibodies to it. The HIV test detects whether antibodies to HIV are in your system.

The initial test that screens for HIV is called EIA, or enzyme immunoassay. Another test, usually the Western blot, confirms one or more positive reactions of the EIA.

The HIV test is very accurate. Yet if you are concerned about a false positive, a second test will confirm your HIV status.

Testing at a Clinic or Doctor's Office

If you are tested at a doctor's office or clinic, a health care worker will draw a small amount of blood from your arm or take oral fluids from your mouth. This sample will be sent to a laboratory and screened.

Call clinics beforehand to find out what their policies are regarding confidentality, cost, and needing permission.

- At most clinics you can be tested either anonymously or confidentially. If you are tested anonymously, no one at the clinic will know your name or anything about you. You will be given a number, and all your testing information will be kept under that number. If you are tested confidentially, the workers at the clinic where you are tested will know your name, but the information is kept confidential as part of your medical record. In many states, this information is shared with local health departments so people can get proper care.

- The cost of an HIV test can vary. Many clinics offer free screening for HIV, yet others may charge as much as $80.

- Ask whether you need parental permission before you take an HIV test. But most clinics do not require it.

If you have trouble finding a clinic in your area, call your local hospital, health department, or one of the hotlines listed at the back of this book.

Test results generally are available in about two weeks. You may learn your results by returning to the test site. A counselor can give you guidance both before and after testing.

If you are tested at your doctor's office, ask your doctor about the test. He or she can help explain the procedure to you, as well as advise you on HIV prevention and what a positive diagnosis means. Although many doctors will keep your test results confidential, you should ask whether or not the doctor will notify your parents of your results.

The HIV Home Test

You also can obtain a kit to test yourself at home. You can buy one at a pharmacy, clinic, or directly from the manufacturer. They cost about $50. Once you take the kit home, read the directions carefully.

A testing kit will include a small lancet and filter paper. You prick your finger with the lancet and put a few drops of blood on the filter paper. Then, using a mailing envelope included in the kit, you mail the paper to a laboratory for testing.

About a week later you can call a toll-free number to obtain your results. You are identified only by a three-digit ID code. A prerecorded message will notify you of a negative result. Positive results will be given by a counselor who will then refer you to resources in your area.

If you look around carefully, you will find a testing procedure that feels right for you.

Chapter 5

When You Are HIV-Positive

*W*hen Shawn learned she was HIV-positive, she had no idea what to do. She was too scared to tell her parents or even her best friend. And she panicked that she was going to get sick and die of AIDS any minute.

Shawn felt hopeless about the future. She would lie awake in bed every night worrying about what was going to happen to her.

Toby learned he had HIV when he was tested during AIDS awareness week at school. He was furious. He was pretty sure he had contracted HIV from his friend Josh, whom he had shared drugs with last year. He wanted to go to Josh's house and beat him up. Instead he went home and screamed at his sister when she asked him what was up.

Chris didn't know how to tell his parents he was HIV-positive. They would want to know how he had contracted it. Chris was in a relationship with another guy, but he had kept it a secret from his parents because they felt strongly that homosexuality was wrong. If Chris told his parents he had gotten HIV from homosexual intercourse, they might throw him out of the house. Then where would he go?

Chris was starting to feel that he deserved to get HIV because he was gay.

Your Emotions

Learning that you are HIV-positive can come as a shock. You will go through many different emotions.

If you can recognize your emotions and find ways to cope with them, it will be easier for you to live with HIV.

- **anger:** like Toby, many people get angry when they learn they have HIV. Often that anger is toward the person who gave them HIV. It's normal to be angry. But be careful that your anger does not get misdirected. For example, instead of understanding his anger, Toby went home and blew up at his sister.

- **guilt and shame:** Chris felt guilty that he had HIV, that he deserved it. He also was scared to tell his parents about his sexual orientation.

    Because he felt he had no one to turn to, he turned his feelings inward. As a result, he felt ashamed of who he was.

Having HIV brings up many issues that you may not feel comfortable talking about with your parents. This is true especially if they are not aware that you are sexually active or have used drugs. While this may be difficult, there are ways you can work through it. Consider speaking with a professional counselor or joining a support group. They help give you the tools you need to talk about your HIV status with others.

Counseling also may help you overcome your feelings of guilt and shame. No one deserves to get HIV. HIV is not a punishment, no matter how you got it.

- **fear and depression:** Shawn reacted with fear. She felt as if she were going to die any minute. She also was depressed, losing hope for the future.

  Nearly everyone is afraid of illness and death. But don't panic that HIV will strike you down. It changes your life forever, but life doesn't stop as soon as you find out you have HIV. You can lead a long, happy, and productive life and still have HIV.

  Worrying about illness can actually help bring sickness on. You are more likely to have stress-related disorders such as insomnia, stomach problems, and headaches. Constant worry also wears down your immune system, which you want to avoid if you have HIV.

  Sadness and fear are normal. But be sure that

there is a person, or group of people, with whom
you can share your feelings. Keeping your worries
to yourself will make them worse.

Coping with Feelings

There are many ways to cope with the emotions that
you feel when you are HIV-positive. As mentioned
before, you may benefit from counseling, either one-
on-one or with a group of other HIV-positive teens.
You may find out about counseling options through
your doctor, local clinic, your insurance company (if
you are covered by insurance), or through any of the
organizations listed at the back of this book.

Find out as much as you can about HIV and AIDS.
Read books on the subject. Read the newspaper and
collect pamphlets that will keep you up-to-date on new
developments on HIV treatment. Talk with others
about how they have handled their diagnosis. Staying
in touch with others will help you understand your
own feelings.

Chapter 6

Treating HIV and AIDS

As you know, there are promising new treatments for HIV and AIDS. But you can do a lot to help yourself by taking care of your body and mind.

Good Nutrition

It's important to eat healthy foods when you are HIV-positive so that your immune system stays strong. You also will want to modify your diet slightly because you have new nutritional needs.

Increase your meat intake so that it makes up about one-fourth of your diet. This will help replenish an essential vitamin, B-12, and cholesterol, both of which are depleted by HIV. If you are a vegetarian, ask your doctor about taking supplements. Also, drink plenty of water—at least two quarts a day.

Eating fruits and vegetables is important. Yet you

must make sure to wash vegetables thoroughly and cook them to kill bacteria. Likewise, peel fruits to remove bacteria and chemicals.

Try to prevent weight loss. If you find you are losing weight, you can drink calorie-rich liquid supplements that are available at grocery stores.

There are also foods to avoid. They include sugar, which may encourage the virus to grow, and white flour, which is difficult to digest. Also avoid pork, which may carry harmful bacteria. And do not eat rare meat, raw fish, or raw eggs, because they also carry bacteria.

Exercise

Exercise can help you stay healthy, whether or not you are HIV-positive. Even if you just take a walk, you are keeping your body strong. Exercise also releases endorphins, body chemicals that relieve pain and increase your sense of well-being.

Don't set a very strict regimen for yourself. But a semi-regular workout schedule will help you both physically and emotionally.

Going to the Doctor

A soon as you know you are HIV-positive, plan how you will handle your medical needs. If you have a primary care physician, make an appointment with him or her to talk about your HIV status.

Make sure that you understand what your doctor tells you. If something sounds unclear, it's okay to ask for more explanation. It helps to bring someone with

you to your appointments. A friend or parent can be a
good person to talk things over with and ask the doc-
ctor questions, too.

Write down any questions you have in advance.
That way, if you are nervous, you won't forget to ask
anything. And during the appointment, write down
the answers to your questions.

Also ask your doctor about how much treatment
will cost. Based on what your doctor tells you, you
may decide to work out a payment plan. Or you can
be referred to another clinic or treatment center that
has lower fees.

If your doctor is impatient with you, or if you feel
uncomfortable with him or her, consider switching
doctors. A doctor's job is to help you, not to make you
more stressed.

Medications to Treat HIV and AIDS

Prevention of HIV is the best way to control the epidemic. You can prevent yourself from acquiring HIV,
you can keep from spreading it, and you can help prevent many AIDS-related illnesses through diet, exercise, and rest. But if you are HIV-positive, you also
will take one or many forms medication.

As to when your treatment will start—it depends.
Your doctor will regularly check the level of T cells,
the cells in your immune system that HIV attacks.
Some treatments begin when T cells drop below 500.
Other doctors may start you on medication earlier,
when your T-cell count is higher.

Another way to identify the level of HIV in your body is through the RNA PCR test. This is called the "viral load" test because it measures the amount of HIV in your system. Some doctors believe that HIV treatment should aim to keep your viral load under 5,000.

There are many medications to treat HIV. You most likely will take a number of them in combination. Doctors have found that this method of treatment, called combination therapy, works more effectively than taking a single medicine. There are three different kinds of drugs used in combination therapy: nucleoside analogs, protease inhibitors, and non-nucleoside reverse transcriptase inhibitors.

When you are taking medicine, *it is extremely important that you stay on schedule.* Follow directions carefully, and devise a system that will help you take your medicine on time. Write down a daily schedule and stick to it. You most likely will have to take different medicines at different times during the day. If you do not take your medicine on time, HIV may become resistant to the medicine.

Before you start a new medicine, ask your doctor about its side effects. Most medications for HIV have side effects, some of which are serious. Be aware of how your body reacts to drugs, and report any side effects you experience to your doctor.

Combination therapy is a lot of work. But the results so far have been very promising. While it does not work for everyone, combination therapy has slowed down the progression of HIV in many people. Doctors and patients are waiting to see what the long-term results of combination therapy will be.

There also are other treatments for HIV, including the use of experimental drugs. Ask your doctor about alternative treatments that are open to you.

Identifying Some Opportunistic Infections
There are illnesses that you may experience when you are HIV-positive. Ask your doctor for information on symptoms and treatments of:

- thrush (mouth fungus)
- oral hairy leukoplakia (patches of fine hair on the tongue)
- herpes zoster
- certain types of pneumonia
- tuberculosis
- toxoplasmosis
- Kaposi's sarcoma
- cervical cancer

Many of the above illnesses can be prevented or treated when they come up. So it's very important that you stay aware of your health and stay in touch with your doctor.

When Someone You Love Has HIV or AIDS
By the year 2000, nearly every person in the United

States will know someone who is HIV-positive. So even when you do not have HIV or AIDS, it's important to know as much as you can about them.

You can help someone who is HIV-positive by loving and accepting him or her. Many people react with fear when they hear about HIV or AIDS. They are afraid that they are going to get it, or they're afraid of the emotions and responsibilities of helping someone who is sick.

You already know that you can't get HIV by having casual contact with a person. Unless you have unprotected sexual intercourse with your friend or share his or her drug needles, you will not get HIV from him or her.

It's true that a person with HIV or AIDS, especially if he or she is ill, may at some time need help with some responsibilities such as transportation and grocery shopping. It's up to you to decide how you can help. Tell your friend what you can do, as well as what you can't. Sometimes a person with HIV just needs to know that you care. Keep the lines of communication open.

Looking To the Future

Especially now that there are new ways to manage HIV and treat AIDS-related illnesses, the future for curing AIDS looks more hopeful that it ever has before.

But there still is a long way to go. Researchers still have not discovered a successful cure for, or vaccine against, HIV. So prevention continues to be the only way to end the HIV epidemic.

By learning about HIV and AIDS and taking care of yourself, you can help keep your future bright.

Glossary

acquired immunodeficiency syndrome An
incurable disease when the immune system has
been damaged by HIV (human immunodeficiency
virus) and is unable to fight infection.

AIDS Abbreviation of acquired immunodeficiency
syndrome.

antibody proteins in the blood that recognize and
block foreign substances and infections.

AZT (zidovudine, retrovir) The first and one of
the most common drugs used to treat HIV.

B cell A cell that makes antibodies to fight infection.

blood donors People who give some of their blood
to a blood bank to be used for a transfusion.

combination therapy The use of two or more
drugs during treatment for HIV.

condom A flexible rubber protective device that is
placed over the penis before sexual intercourse. It
can prevent pregnancy and the spread of disease.

disease A group of physical problems usually caused by an organism.

drug abusers People who use drugs to change the way they feel, not to make themselves well.

gay Homosexual.

hemophilia An inherited disease that makes people unable to stop bleeding when they are cut or scraped.

heterosexual Someone who chooses members of the opposite sex for romantic or sexual relationships.

homosexual Someone who chooses members of the same sex for romantic or sexual relationships.

semen Sperm-carrying fluid released through the penis at the climax of sexual activity.

sexual intercourse Sexual contact between people involving the entry of the penis into the vagina or other private parts of the sexual partner.

side effects The action or effect of a drug other than that which is desired. The term usually refers to negative or undesirable effects, such as headache, nausea, or rash.

symptom A physical change or feeling in the body (fever, cough, bleeding, tiredness, sleeplessness) that is not usual and that doctors know to be a sign of a disease.

syndrome A group of symptoms that indicate a certain disease.

T cell A cell in the blood that tells B cells to make antibodies. HIV kills T cells.

transfusion A transfer of a liquid, usually blood, into the bloodstream.

transmission The process of spreading a germ and the infection caused by that germ.

vaccine Medicine given to a person by a doctor to increase immunity to a particular disease.

vein A part of the body through which blood flows.

virus Any of a large group of small organisms that causes an infection in any living thing.

white blood cells Part of the immune system that protects the body against foreign substances, such as disease-producing microorganisms.

Where to Go for Help

AIDS Treatment Data Network
http://www.aidsnyc.org/network

Division of HIV/AIDS Prevention
Centers for Disease Control and Prevention
National AIDS Hotline: (800) 342-AIDS
Spanish: (800) 344-7432
TTY: (800) 243-7889
Web site: http://www.cdc.gov/nchstp/hiv_aids/dhap.htm
e-mail: hivmail@cdc.gov

Gay Men's Health Crisis
129 West 20th Street
New York, NY 10011
(212) 807-6655
(212) 645-7470 (TTY)
Web site: http:/www.gmhc.org

HIV/AIDS Treatment Information Service
(800) 448-0440 (Voice)
(800) 243-7012 (TTY)
(301) 519-6616
Web site: http://www.hivatis.org/
e-mail: atis@cdcnac.org

**Immunet: Easy Access to Quality Information
about HIV/AIDS**
Web site: http://www.immunet.org/

National Clearinghouse for Alcohol and Drug Information
P.O. Box 2345
Rockville, MD 20847-2345
(301) 468-2600
(800) 729-6686
Web site: http://www.health.org/
e-mail: info@health.org

National Hemophilia Foundation
110 Greene St., Ste. 303
New York, NY 10012
(212) 219-8180

Office of Civil Rights
U.S. Department of Health and Human Services
P.O. Box 13716
Philadelphia, PA 19101

In Canada

AIDS Vancouver
1272 Richard Street
Vancouver, British Columbia V6B 3G2
(604) 687-2437

AIDS Network of Edmonton Society
#201 11456 Jasper Avenue
Edmonton, Alberta T5K 0MI
(403) 488-5742

Metro Area Committee on AIDS (MACAIDS)
5675 Spring Garden Road
Suite 305
Halifax, Nova Scotia B3J 1H1
(902) 425-4882

For Further Reading

Arrick, Fran. *What You Don't Know Can Kill You.*
    New York: Bantam, 1992.

Draimin, Barbara Hermie. *Drugs and AIDS.* New
    York: The Rosen Publishing Group. Rev. ed. 1997.

Ford, Michael Thomas. *100 Questions and Answers
    About AIDS: What You Need to Know.* New
    York: William Morrow & Co., 1993.

Ford, Michael Thomas. *The Voices of AIDS: Twelve
    Unforgettable People Talk About How AIDS Has
    Changed Their Lives.* New York: William Morrow
    & Co., 1996.

Glass, George. *Drugs and Fitting In.* New York: The
    Rosen Publishing Group, 1998.

Johnson, Earvin "Magic." *What You Can Do to Avoid
    AIDS.* New York: Times Books, 1992.

Kittredge. Mary, and Dale C. Garrell. *Teens with AIDS
    Speak Out.* Englewood Cliffs, NJ: Julian Messner,
    1992.

Moe, Barbara. *Everything You Need to Know About Sexual Abstinence.* New York: The Rosen Publishing Group. Rev. ed. 1998.

Rubenstein, William, B. *The Rights of People Who Are HIV-Positive.* Carbondale, IL: Southern Illinois Press, 1996.

Index

A

abstinence, 22, 34
AIDS, 6-7, 14, 16, 24
    and children, 24, 39
    consequences, 7
    defined, 7, 9-15
    preventing, 7, 38, 50, 54
    protection from, 7, 10, 38
    related illnesses, 52-53
    symptoms, 7, 14
    talking about, 30-34
    treating, 48-54
antibodies, 13, 41

B

bacteria, 44

B cells, 12-13
birth control, 24, 33
blood, 16-17, 19
    transfusion, 24-26
blood cells, 12
    platelets, 12
    red, 12
    white, 12

C

Centers for Disease Control
    and Prevention, 8, 24
clinics, 40, 41-43, 47
communication, 30-34, 54
condoms, 22, 29-30, 32, 33
counseling, 46, 47

D

doctors, 40, 41, 47, 49-50, 51-52
drug abuse, 7, 16, 17-20, 27,
    32, 34-35, 46

E

emotions, 45, 47
    anger, 45
    depression, 46-47
    fear, 46-47
    guilt, 45-46
endorphins, 49
Enzyme Immunoassay (EIA),
    41
exercise, 49

H

help, 53-54
hemophiliacs, 24-26
heroin, 19-20
herpes, 32
HIV, 7, 8, 10, 13
    and children, 22, 39
    contracting, 16-26, 32, 34,
    36
    defined, 7
    diagnosing, 14
    lliving with, 43-47
    parents with, 22-24, 38-39
    preventing, 27-35, 50
    "spiking," 14
    testing for, 13, 26, 32, 36-
    43, 51
    transmitting, 7, 16-26, 29,
    33, 38-39, 50

    treatment of, 14, 47, 48-54
homosexuals, 27

I

immune system, 7, 9, 10-15,
    22, 35, 46, 48
infection, 13, 14, 16
intravenous drug use, 17-20,
    34, 38

K

Kaposi's sarcoma, 9, 53

M

medicines, 7, 50-52
mucous membranes, 16, 20, 21

N

needles, 7, 19-20, 53
nutrition, 48-49

P

parents, 22-24, 38-39, 40, 50
pneumonia, 9, 52
pre-seminal fluid, 21
protecting yourself, 7, 8, 16

R

rectum, 21

S

semen, 16, 21
sexual abuse, 38
sexual intercourse, 7, 16, 20-
    22, 29-30, 32-34, 38, 53
sexually transmitted diseases,

                32, 40   viruses, 7, 8, 12, 21, 41
stress, 46, 50   defined, 10
                                      growth of, 10
T
T cells, 12, 13, 50-51   **W**
teens, 8   Western blot, 41

V
vaccines, 13, 54

About the Author
Barbara Taylor is a writer/editor at *Weekly Reader* in
Middletown, Connecticut. She has taught in Japan, France, and
Germany, as well as in elementary classrooms in
Massachusetts.

Acknowledgments and Photo Credits
Cover photo by Stuart Rabinowitz; p. 2 © H. Armstrong
Roberts; p. 12 © Science Pictures Limited/Corbis; p. 15 ©
Sygma/Jane Rosett; p. 18 by Blackbirch Graphics; p. 20 ©
Annie Griffiths Belt/Corbis; p. 23 by Ira Fox; p. 25 © Paul A.
Souders/Corbis; p. 30 © Sygma/A. Tannenbaum; p. 33 by
Megan Alderson; p. 53 © AP/Wide World Photos; p. 56 ©
Sygma/Thierry Orban